YOU SPEAK, THEY ACT :
How to influence anyone's decision with effective Manipulation tactics

Alice Tallman

Table of contents

Chapter One: The Concept Of Influence

Definition of influence:

When it comes to motivating their team members and ensuring that everyone is working toward the same goal, successful leaders often rely on their influence and ability to persuade others to utilize their abilities. There are distinctions to be made between the leadership qualities of persuasion and influence, even though both are necessary. Learning how to enhance your persuasive abilities and grow your influence may be of interest to you if you want to be a successful leader in your business and you have aspirations of reaching that goal.

The power to directly impact the behaviors, choices, views, or thoughts of other people is what we mean when we talk about having influence.In the end, having influence enables one to get things done and accomplish goals in a manner that is satisfactory to them.

On the most fundamental level, influence is about compliance, or persuading someone to act in a way that is following your desires (or at least not undermining them). But the true dedication of other people is often necessary for you to be able to achieve important objectives and complete important activities.

A person's identity includes their level of influence on others. Influence is often gained by individuals as a result of their achievements, behaviors, or social standing. It may be simpler for professionals who influence to convince other people to agree with them, collaborate with them toward the achievement of a certain objective, or pursue the required course of action.

The following are some abilities that may assist you in increasing your level of influence:

Interpersonal skills

Increasing your level of proficiency in interpersonal communication may help you become more self-assured and enable you to feel more at ease while participating in face-to-face exchanges with other individuals. Strong interpersonal skills may make it simpler for professionals to begin discussions, establish rapport, and connect with people on a meaningful level. This is especially true when it comes to networking.

Pay attention to how other individuals in your company communicate with each other and make a mental note of the people whose good attributes you respect. Doing so will help you develop your interpersonal abilities. After that, give some attention to how you might enhance your relations with other people.

Participating in interesting activities, such as going to the theatre, seeing stand-up comedy, or attending events for networking, may also help you improve your interpersonal skills while providing you with opportunities to have fun and meet new people.

Abilities in communication

You may hone your ability to persuade others and expand your sphere of influence over time by developing your communication abilities to a high level. Practice articulating your thoughts in a way that is clear, succinct, and easily understood by others by using language and a vocabulary that is straightforward and uncomplicated. This will help you develop a strong communication skill set.

When communicating with other people, you should also pay attention to the expressions on your face, the movements you make, and the tone of your voice. This may help you interact with other people and ensure that your nonverbal indications are consistent with the remarks you make.

Using logic and deduction to reach a conclusion

Providing evidence that backs up your statements with logical and deductive reasoning will help you construct more compelling and convincing arguments. Before you provide your counsel, you should first carefully consider the circumstances at hand and do some in-depth reflection on the options available to you.

You might also study a certain subject before becoming involved in a discussion to ensure that you are well-versed in the subject matter and possess the information necessary to present a balanced perspective.

You may improve your ability to think logically and reason deductively by engaging in creative activities, such as puzzles or games that require you to find solutions to problems. You may also strengthen your research abilities by getting in the habit of questioning things that come up in the course of your everyday life. This will help you evaluate problems from a variety of angles.

Emotional intelligence

Another essential ability is having a keen awareness of the feelings of others and the ability to accurately interpret those feelings. If you have a high degree of emotional intelligence, it will be easier for you to connect with other people, personalize your communication, and establish trust.

Observe the facial expressions and other nonverbal indicators that other people use to communicate their thoughts and feelings, and pay careful attention to how they respond. For instance, if someone crosses their arms, gives brief replies, and constantly looks around the room, this may be an indication that they are bored in the discussion that you are having with them.

In this situation, if you wish to reengage the person you're conversing with, you can try changing the tone of your voice or moving on to a different subject. Improving your emotional intelligence may be accomplished by demonstrating empathy for other people and making an effort to comprehend the emotions that motivate and drive them.

Negotiation skills

When you have excellent negotiating abilities, it will be easier for you to come to an agreement with other people, convince them to agree with you, and apply strategy to the talks you have. Determine what it is that the other person places importance on, what their requirements are, and how they may profit by agreeing with you.

This might assist you in developing a more persuasive argument that is tailored to the individual with whom you are now conversing. Your ability to negotiate effectively may be improved by showing that you are prepared to compromise or by giving alternate proposals that can still assist you in achieving your objective.

Participatory listening

When you are discussing with other people, it might be beneficial to pay attention to what they are saying and actively listen to what they are saying since this can help you establish common ground, make more persuasive arguments, and enhance your communication. Do not interrupt the other people who are taking part in the chat while they are attempting to give their perspectives.

This will not only make them feel heard but will also demonstrate that you appreciate their views. It will also help you understand what inspires them. You may demonstrate that you are listening by maintaining eye contact with the person or by nodding your head at suitable times.

When it is your moment to speak, make an effort to support your position by repeating portions of what they said in your answer. You may do this by appealing to the reasons and values that they have.
Why do you think having influence is so important?

You may sway the opinions of others and earn the respect of those who are close to them by arguing your case. In any setting, influence may be seen as a sort of power, but this is particularly true in the workplace. People who influence the workplace are often more trusted and acknowledged by their peers. Additionally, prominent individuals are often also better at leading others.

The ability to wield influence or persuasion effectively is a potent instrument that is essential to organizational life. Even better would be to make good use of it to successfully carry out duties and accomplish objectives. A strong instrument for assuring one's success inside an organization is being skilled in the art of influence and using it effectively. Of

Chapter Two: Self Analysis

Definition Of Self Analysis:

Self-analysis is a process in which a person makes an effort to learn about and comprehend themselves to investigate the likelihood of changing their nature, personality, and the driving forces behind their actions.

For someone like myself, who is always curious about everything and everything, it is not uncommon for that person to wonder about themselves. This question, on the other hand, might be a great hardship for someone who blindly accepts everything they are told and taught.

What exactly is self-analysis, then?
I was looking for a definition of self-analysis when I came across this one: "the examination of oneself, in particular one's reasons and character." In addition, I was rather aback to discover this, given that I had anticipated discovering something philosophical or extradimensional instead. I didn't feel that this term covered everything, so I looked for further resources on the topic. Then there was this one, which defined it as "a methodical endeavour by an individual to comprehend his or her personality without the assistance of another person." It's so freezing... Isn't it? And I wondered what's wrong with this search engine today. Because every time I asked something as basic as, "What nail colour should I put on?" it offered me such profound insights that I forgot to put nail colour on my nails. And when I'm inquiring

about something as interesting as "Self-Analysis," that's when I know I'm being chilly. But I couldn't quit because it made me even more inquisitive about why people don't talk about a subject that is as significant as this one. Also, I came upon a book written by L. Ron Hubbard titled "Self Analysis." So, I ordered it. Because I am a genuine impatient creature, I attempted to research this topic before the arrival of this book. And in this regard, I have developed my definition of it...

"Self-analysis is a process in which a person strives to know and understand oneself to investigate potential modifications that might be inferred in one's character, personality, and motivations,"

If I had to be honest, I would say that I am not yet pleased (God, I wonder when this book will come!). You may be wondering what the problem is with the two definitions that I described before. My brain couldn't wrap itself around the first one because it was too straightforward and it was a dictionary definition, but the second one made me question whether or not I should agree with the first. It specifically states "without the assistance of another individual." I don't believe anybody has ever attempted self-analysis without the assistance of another individual. In the process of self-analysis, assistance from another person is always required, regardless of whether it is direct or indirect.

Self-analysis is a process that takes place inside a person; nevertheless, you are unable to complete it on your own unless you are a person who is 100 per cent honest with yourself, which is not always the case for any of us. Self-analysis requires us to consider ourselves as if we were looking at ourselves from the point of view of another person. If we rely just on our judgment, we will never be able to conduct an accurate and thorough self-analysis. Even if we have the opinion that a certain aspect of our conduct is positive, this does not guarantee that it is so from the perspective of another person. Even if we have good intentions and believe they will lead to success, there is no guarantee that others will share our perspectives. Therefore, doing a self-analysis is a procedure that is motivated by the want to learn more about oneself from the point of view of a collective of other people.

Why is it necessary to do so?
The first thing one should do while working toward achieving a goal, a target, or a certain level of achievement is to analyze themselves. Because the path begins with each of us individually. Self-analysis provides us with a plan to follow on our journey toward being the sort of people we most want to be. Because it provides a gateway to contemplate both ourselves and everything else that has contributed to our development into the people we are now.

When we conduct an in-depth examination of ourselves, we become aware of every aspect of our being that, for us to develop, calls for modification or enhancement.

The first step toward self-love and progress is doing an in-depth investigation of oneself. And development requires both of these things. It provides clarity to our thoughts so that we can think on the appropriate path. We have a propensity to concentrate more on how to get a favourable result with all of the personality features that we have. Even when we see unfavourable characteristics in the personalities of others, we make an effort to rationalize such aspects by our actions, which leads to improved communication in our social circles and at work. Through doing self-analysis, we can become more aware of our deeds, statements, and motivations. And the practice of mindfulness is essential to achieving inner calm and joy.

Chapter Three: Analyzing People

The truth about someone cannot be deduced just from their logical reasoning. To develop your ability to interpret the essential non-verbal intuition signals that others emit, you will need to make peace with the fact that there are other significant sources of information. To do this, you need to be prepared to let go of any preconceived notions as well as any emotional baggage, such as long-standing grudges or ego conflicts, that prevent you from seeing someone in their true light. The most important thing is to maintain an impartial stance and take in information in an unprejudiced manner without altering it.

Certain barriers need to come down. Despite how well-developed one's brain may be, one must always be prepared to abandon outmoded concepts.

People who are skilled at reading people are also skilled at reading what is unseen. They have learnt to harness what I refer to as their "super-senses" to look farther than where you typically place your attention to have access to intuitive ideas that may change their lives. In my book, "The Ecstasy of Surrender," I discuss a variety of approaches to reading people. I encourage you to experiment with some of these approaches. They all demand abandoning pure logic in favour of accepting alternate and non-linear types of input in addition to the traditional form of data.

The art of reading people may be broken down into three distinct steps.
The first method is to pay attention to nonverbal cues such as body language.

According to research, words only account for seven percent of how we communicate, however our body language (fifty-five percent) and voice tone (thirty percent) account for the remaining percentages. In this situation, the surrender that you should concentrate on is letting go of straining too hard to comprehend the signs provided by body language. Avoid being too serious or analytical. Maintain a state of calm and fluidity. Make yourself at home, relax, and concentrate on taking it all in.

1. Give Careful Consideration to Your Appearance

When reading the works of others, observe: Are they dressed for success, giving off the impression that they are ambitious by donning a power suit and well-polished shoes? What better way to show that you're comfortable than by wearing jeans and a T-shirt? Is it a tempting decision to wear a skintight shirt with cleavage? A pendant that communicates one's spiritual beliefs, such as a cross or a Buddha?

2. Notice Posture

Ask yourself this question while analyzing the posture of other people: Do they carry themselves with a sense of self-assurance? Or, as an indication of poor self-esteem, do they stroll indecisively or crouch when confronted? Do they go about with their chest pushed up, which is an indication of having a large ego?

3. Keep an eye out for any visible movements.

Observe where people lean and how far apart they are standing. In general, we gravitate toward individual whose company we like and avoid those whose company we do not enjoy.
Arms and legs crossed is a posture that conveys defensiveness, rage, or a desire to

protect oneself from harm. People have a tendency, when they cross their legs, to point the toes of the upper leg towards the direction of the person with whom they feel the most comfortable.

Hiding one's hands — It gives the impression that a person is trying to conceal something when they place their hands on their laps, put them in their pockets, or put them behind their backs.

When individuals bite their lips, lick their lips, or pick at their cuticles, they are attempting to calm themselves when they are under pressure or when they are in an embarrassing circumstance.

4. Interpret Facial Expression

Emotions can leave permanent marks on our faces. The appearance of deep frown lines may indicate concern or excessive pondering. The smiling lines known as crow's feet are caused by happiness. A symbol of rage, scorn, or bitterness is having your lips drawn together. Both clenching one's jaw and grinding one's teeth are telltale indicators of strain.

The second method is to pay attention to the guidance provided by your intuition.

You can understand someone by paying attention to more than just their words and body language. What your gut tells you rather than what your intellect tells you is intuition. More often than not, the information that comes to you in the form of visuals and a-ha moments is nonverbal. If you want to get to know someone, you have to go beyond their outward appearance and focus on who they are on the inside. Your intuition enables you to look beyond the apparent and uncover a more compelling narrative.

1. Pay Attention to Your Instincts

Pay attention to what your instincts tell you, particularly during the first encounter. It's an instinctive response that happens even before you've had a chance to think about it. It communicates whether or not you are feeling at ease. Feelings in one's gut are an immediate and primordial reaction. They serve as an internal truth meter for you, indicating whether or not you can trust other people.

2. You should get the chills.

The sensation of having goosebumps is a wonderful intuitive tingling that occurs when we connect with individuals who move or inspire us or when they say something that strikes a chord in us. You may also get goosebumps when you have deja-vu, which is the feeling that you have known someone in the past even though you have never really met them.

3. Keep an eye out for sudden flashes of insight.

During chats, you could have an "ah-ha" moment while thinking about folks who appear out of nowhere. Keep a level head. If you don't pay attention, you could miss it. Because we have a propensity to move on to the next thought so quickly, we frequently fail to retain important insights.

4. Be on the lookout for innate empathy.

A severe kind of empathy is when you can experience the physical symptoms and feelings of another person in your own body. This may happen at times. When you talk to others, keep this question in mind: "Does my back ache now when it didn't before? Am I sad or irritated after an unremarkable meeting?" Get comments to judge whether or not this demonstrates empathy.

The third method is to pick up on people's emotional energy.

Emotions are a magnificent manifestation of our energy or the "vibe" that we put out into the world. These are things that come to us via our intuition. Being with some individuals makes you feel wonderful; they boost both your mood and your vigour. When you're with other people, it saps your energy and makes you want to run away. Even though it cannot be seen, this "subtle energy" may be felt a few inches or feet away from the body. It is referred to as chi in traditional Chinese medicine. Chi is a vitality that plays an important role in maintaining overall health.

Techniques for Interpreting Emotional Energy

1. Be aware of the presence of other people

This is the energy that we give out as a whole, which may or may not be compatible with our words or actions. It's the mental climate that envelops us like a cloud or a sun, depending on the context. As you read about different individuals, you should pay attention to whether or not they exude a warm and inviting demeanour. Or are you experiencing the chills, which are causing you to retreat?

2. Pay Attention to the Eyes of Others

The eyes are a potent energy transmitter. According to research, the eyes produce an electromagnetic signal much as the brain does, which means that this signal may be detected outside of the body. Spend some time focusing on people's pupils. Do they have any compassion? Sexy? Tranquil? Mean? Angry? Also, check to see whether they seem to have someone at home, which is an indication of their ability to form close relationships. Or do they give off the impression of being guarded or hiding?

3. Pay Attention to How a Hug, a Handshake, and Other Touches Feel

By making physical touch with one another, we exchange emotional energy that is similar to an electrical current. Ask yourself: Does the act of shaking hands or giving a hug make you feel warm, comfortable, and confident. Or does it make you uncomfortable to the point that you want to withdraw? Are the people's palms sweaty, which is a symptom of anxiety? Or flaccid, which connotes hesitancy and lack of commitment?

4. Pay Attention to Your Laughter and Tone of Voice

The pitch, as well as the loudness, of our voice, may reveal a great deal about our state of mind. Vibrations are produced when sound frequencies interact. Pay attention to the effect that a person's tone of voice has on you while reading them. Ask yourself: Does their voice have a calming effect on you? Or does it come out as harsh, sarcastic, or whiny?

Chapter Four: Emotional intelligence

What Is Meant When We Speak About Emotional Intelligence?

Emotional Intelligence

The term "emotional intelligence" (EI) refers to a person's capacity to recognize, manage, and analyze their feelings. While some experts believe that emotional intelligence is a trait that can be developed via training and practice, others maintain that it is a quality that is present from birth.

The capacity to recognize, interpret, and react appropriately to the emotions of others is just as important as the capacity to express and manage one's feelings. Imagine living in a world where you had no way of knowing when a friend or coworker was upset or furious and you were unable to read their emotions. This capacity is referred regarded as emotional intelligence by psychologists, and some experts believe that it may even be more essential than IQ in determining your overall level of success in life.

Signals that a person has emotional intelligence:

The following are some important indicators and instances of emotional intelligence:

1. The capacity to recognize and articulate the emotions that other people are experiencing
2. A conscious understanding of one's capabilities and constraints

3. The power to forgive oneself and move forward from past errors
4. The capacity to acknowledge and welcome change The possession of a

strong sense of curiosity, especially towards other people
5. Feelings of empathy and care for others
6. Having empathy for the experiences and sentiments of other individuals
7. Taking ownership of one's actions and learning from them
8. The capacity to maintain emotional composure amid difficult circumstances

The Methods Used to Assess Emotional Intelligence

Several distinct tests have been developed in recent years to determine a person's degree of emotional intelligence. These kinds of examinations may often be broken down into one of two categories: self-report examinations or ability examinations.

The most popular kind of exam is a self-report test since it is both simple to give and straightforward to assess. During these types of examinations, respondents provide ratings of their actions in response to questions or remarks. For instance, a test-taker might respond to a statement like "I often feel that I understand how others are feeling" by indicating that they disagree with the statement, that they somewhat disagree with the statement, that they agree with the statement, or that they strongly agree with the statement.

On the other hand, ability tests evaluate a person's talents by seeing how they react to a variety of scenarios after which they are graded. People are often required to show their talents through these types of examinations, which are subsequently scored by an impartial party.

If you are participating in a test of emotional intelligence that is being given by a mental health professional, the following two measures may be utilized:

Mayer-Salovey-Caruso The Emotional Intelligence Test, often known as the MSCEIT, is a capability-based assessment that examines each of the four components that make up Mayer and Salovey's EI paradigm. Participants in the examination do exercises meant to evaluate their capacity to recognize, categorize, comprehend, and control their feelings.

The Emotional and Social Competence Inventory (ESCI), which is based on an older instrument known as the Self-Assessment Questionnaire, asks people who are familiar with the individual to rate that person's abilities in many different emotional competencies. The results of these ratings are then compiled and analyzed. The purpose of the exam is to determine whether or not an individual has the social and emotional capabilities that are indicative of great leadership.

There are also a lot of less formal tools available online, and most of them are free.

These may be used to study your emotional intelligence.

How To Perform Emotional Intelligence Tests On Yourself.

Emotional Intelligence: The Parts That Make It Up

According to the findings of recent studies, there may be as many as four distinct levels of emotional intelligence. These levels include the ability to perceive emotions, the capacity to reason using emotions, the capacity to comprehend emotions, and the capacity to regulate emotions.

Having an accurate perception of one's emotions is the first step in developing a comprehension of those feelings. This may need a comprehension of nonverbal cues like body language and facial emotions in many different scenarios.

Emotional reasoning is the next level, which entails making use of one's feelings to stimulate thinking and other cognitive pursuits. Emotions play a role in the prioritization of what we pay attention to and how we react; we have emotional responses to things that catch our attention.

An understanding of emotions is necessary since the feelings that we experience may be interpreted in a great number of different ways. When someone is showing furious feelings, it is the observer's responsibility to decipher the reasons behind the person's wrath and what it may indicate. For instance, if your employer is behaving irate, it may indicate that they are unhappy with the job that you have done. However, it is also possible that they are upset because they received a ticket for speeding on their way to work that morning or that they have been arguing with their spouse.

Emotional control: The capacity to properly control one's emotions is an essential component of emotional intelligence and represents the greatest degree of this trait. Emotional management entails many essential components, including the ability to control one's feelings, react properly, and comprehend and respond to the feelings of others.

This model's four different branches are structured hierarchically, with the simpler processes being located at the lower levels and the more complicated processes being located at the higher levels. For instance, feeling and expressing emotion are included at the lowest levels, but controlling the feelings and feelings of others is involved in the upper levels, which need more conscious engagement.

Emotional Intelligence Comprises These 5 Key Components

1. The Influence of One's Level of Emotional Intelligence

In recent years, there has been a rising interest in both the teaching of and the development of social and emotional intelligence. Programs that focus on students' social and emotional development have been included in the curricula of an increasing number of schools.

The purpose of these efforts is not only to promote health and well-being among students but also to assist students in achieving academic success and to discourage bullying behaviour among students. There are several situations in which emotionally intelligent behaviour may be of use in one's day-to-day existence.

2. Considering All Options Before Acting

Emotionally knowledgeable people are aware that feelings might be strong, but they can also be fleeting. When an emotionally charged event occurs, such as being upset with a coworker, an emotionally intelligent reaction would be to take some time before reacting. An example of this would be becoming angry with a coworker. Everyone involved will be able to regain control of their emotions and think more sensibly about the myriad of issues surrounding the disagreement as a result of this.

3. A heightened sense of self-awareness

Emotionally intelligent people are not only competent at knowing how other people may feel, but they are also adept at comprehending the sensations that they are experiencing. People can evaluate the myriad of circumstances that play a role in their emotions when they have a healthy level of self-awareness.

4. Concern and Compatibility with Other People

One of the most important aspects of emotional intelligence is the capacity to reflect on and sympathize with the experiences and emotions of others. This requires a lot of people to think about how they would react if they were in the same circumstances as the other person.

5. Others who have a high level of emotional intelligence can take into account the viewpoints, experiences, and feelings of other individuals and then utilize this knowledge to explain why people act in the ways that they do.

How to Put emotional intelligence In Use

Emotional intelligence may be used in a wide variety of contexts and settings in one's everyday life. Developing emotional intelligence may be done in a variety of different methods, including:

1. Being able to take in constructive criticism as well as personal responsibility
2. Being able to put an error in the past and move on with life
3. Being able to refuse something when it's necessary and being able to communicate how you feel to other people
4. Having the ability to find solutions to challenges that are acceptable to all parties involved
5. Having compassion and understanding for other people
6. Having exceptional listening abilities
7. Understanding the motivations behind your actions and avoiding passing judgment on those of others
8. It is impossible to have effective interpersonal communication without emotional intelligence. Experts are divided on whether or not intelligence alone is the most essential factor in determining one's level of success in

life. You are in luck since there are activities that you may participate in to improve both your social and emotional intelligence.

9. Gaining an understanding of emotions may be the key to bettering one's relationships, enhancing one's well-being, and improving one's ability to communicate.

Advice on How to Raise Your Level of Emotional Intelligence

Even if some individuals may be born with innate emotional intelligence, there is mounting evidence to show that this is a talent that can be cultivated and improved. For instance, a study that was conducted in 2019 using a randomized control group indicated that training in emotional intelligence might increase emotional talents in professional situations. 3

It's crucial to have emotional intelligence, but how can you develop your own social and emotional skills? What are some actions you may take? Here are some tips.

Listen

The first thing you need to do if you want to comprehend the emotions that other people are experiencing is to pay attention to them. Make it a point to pay attention to what others are trying to tell you, both orally and non-verbally, and to give them the time and attention they need. There is a lot of significance that can be conveyed via body language. When you get the impression that someone is experiencing a certain emotion, you should think about the many things that may be contributing to that experience.

Empathize

It is important to be able to pick up on someone's emotions but to genuinely comprehend their point of view, you also need to be able to put yourself in their shoes and consider things from their perspective. Exercise your capacity to empathize with those around you. Try to picture how you would react if you were in their shoes. These kinds of exercises may assist you in developing a deeper emotional knowledge of a particular circumstance as well as more robust emotional abilities over time.

Reflect

Emotional intelligence includes the capacity to reason with one's feelings, which is an essential component of that intellect. Think about how the feelings you're experiencing right now affect the choices and actions you make. Consider the impact that their feelings have on their behaviour while you are trying to understand how other people will react.

Why does this individual feel the way that they do? Is it possible that certain variables cannot be seen that are contributing to these feelings? How do your feelings compare and contrast with theirs? As you investigate such concerns, you could discover that it gets simpler to comprehend the function that people's feelings play in determining how they think and act.

The 7 Traits That Make Someone Emotionally Intelligent

Potential Pitfalls

A lower level of emotional intelligence abilities may lead to some possible hazards that can influence numerous aspects of a person's life, including their profession and their relationships. These potential pitfalls can have an impact on a variety of situations.

People with less emotional skills tend to engage in more conflicts, have relationships of worse quality, and have poor emotional coping abilities. This is because they have fewer emotional skills.

Having a low degree of emotional intelligence may have a lot of negative consequences, but having a very high level of emotional abilities can also come with its share of difficulties. Take, for instance:

According to some research, those who have a high emotional intelligence may have a lower capacity for creativity and innovation.

People who have a high level of emotional intelligence may have difficulty providing constructive criticism because of a concern that they may offend the emotions of others.

According to the findings of several studies, having a high EQ may sometimes be used for manipulative and dishonest ends.

A Brief Look Back at the Development of Emotional Intelligence

The concept of emotional intelligence did not become common use until sometime around the year 1990. Although it is a relatively new phrase, there has been a remarkable growth in interest in the notion since then.

Early Development

Edward Thorndike, a psychologist, first introduced the concept of "social intelligence" in the 1930s. He defined it as the capacity to get along with other people. In the 1940s, psychologist David Wechsler hypothesized that the many effective components of a person's intellect may play an essential part in determining how successful they are in life. [citation needed]

Later Developments

In the 1950s, a school of thinking known as humanistic psychology began to gain popularity. Proponents of this school of thought, such as Abraham Maslow, placed a greater emphasis on the many ways in which individuals may develop their emotional resilience.

The idea that people might have several bits of intelligence simultaneously is yet another significant concept that arose throughout the process of developing emotional intelligence. In the middle of the 1970s, Howard Gardner came up with the notion that there was more to intelligence than simply a single, overarching talent. He proposed that intelligence included a variety of facets.

The Development of Emotional Intelligence as a Competency

The phrase "emotional intelligence" was not used for the first time until 1985 when it was included in a dissertation written by Wayne Payne for his PhD degree. In an essay written by Keith Beasley and first published in Mensa Magazine in 1987, the phrase "emotional quotient" is used.

The essay "Emotional Intelligence," written by psychologists Peter Salovey and John Mayer and published in the journal Imagination, Cognition, and Personality in 1990, is considered a key work in the field. They described emotional intelligence as "the capacity to monitor one's thoughts and emotions as well as the feelings and emotions of others, to differentiate between them, and to utilize this knowledge to guide one's thinking and actions."

After the release of Daniel Goleman's book titled "Emotional Intelligence: Why It Can Matter More Than IQ" in 1995, the idea of emotional intelligence became well known.

Since then, the concept of emotional intelligence has continued to pique the attention of the general public and has emerged as an essential concept in a variety of disciplines other than psychology, such as education and business.

Chapter Five: Manipulation And Manipulation Tactics

Definition of manipulation.

The term "manipulation" refers to a set of behaviours in the field of psychology that are aimed to exploit, manipulate, or otherwise influence other people for one's benefit.

The definition of the phrase may be different depending on whatever behaviours are particularly mentioned, and these variations are impacted by culture as well as by whether the term is used to refer to the general population or in therapeutic circumstances.
Because it is utilized at the cost of other people, manipulation is often seen as an unethical type of the social influence.

Personality disorders such as borderline personality disorder, narcissistic personality disorder, or antisocial personality disorder may be the root cause of manipulative tendencies.

Manipulation is connected with greater levels of emotional intelligence, and it is a primary component of the personality construct known as Machiavellianism. Both of these findings point to the importance of emotional intelligence.

The terms "general influence" and "persuasion" should not be confused with "manipulation." Because it does not seem to be too forceful and because it respects the right of the one who is being persuaded to accept or reject it, influence is typically considered to be harmless. The ability to drive people to the desired action, often within the framework of a defined purpose, is what we mean when we talk about persuasion. Attempts at persuasion sometimes include trying to change another person's views, faith, motives, or behaviours. In contrast to manipulation, which may only have bad consequences, influence and persuasion have neither positive nor negative connotations.

Any person, in any kind of connection, is susceptible to being manipulated. This includes friendships, romantic partnerships, parent-child ties, and interactions within the extended family. It's possible that anybody at work, including your coworkers and employer, might have manipulative tendencies.

Nevertheless, it is not always easy to spot manipulation.

Manipulation may sometimes be so covert and successful that you may end yourself questioning your perspective of the issue rather than the actions or motivations of the other person. This is because the other person is trying to get you to focus on yourself. The use of gaslighting may make it very difficult to recognize deceptive methods being used.

However, if you are aware of the red flags to watch out for, you may be able to defend yourself from the techniques of manipulation before they even begin.

Recognizing typical forms of psychological manipulation

Manipulative people often resort to using typical manipulation strategies and behaviours to achieve their goals. This is what you should be looking for.

Guilt-tripping

The act of someone trying to make you feel responsible or guilty for the acts or choices you've made is known as "guilt-tripping."

Drake adds that the use of anything that one person has done for the other as "leverage" to obtain what they want is a common form of guilt trip.

The following are some instances of using guilt to gain an advantage:

Lying

People that tend to manipulate others will often lie to control or compel others, as well as to evade responsibility or the repercussions of their actions.

For instance, a youngster who has been warned that they are not permitted to associate with a certain group can fabricate stories about where they have been spending their time. Alternately, they might tell the other parent that they have been granted permission to go out with their pals while in reality, they have not.

Flattery

It is not always easy to differentiate between genuine praise and an attempt at flattery.

When someone truly points out something nice without any expectation of reward, they are offering praise. However, flattery is often used dishonestly as a method for gaining an emotional advantage. When someone flatters you, they often expect that they will get something in return.

For instance, an employee who often compliments their management on their skills and achievements may increase their chances of receiving a raise or promotion.

Projection

A person is said to be engaging in projection when they assert that an emotion that they are experiencing, such as envy, is truly being felt by another individual.

For instance, a person who has a propensity for manipulation could instigate conflict and drama, but then point the finger of blame onto another individual for generating that energy.

Triangulation

Triangulation may take many different forms, but it most often occurs when a third party is dragged into a conversation that should have been kept between the two persons who are directly impacted by the problem.

A manipulative individual could, for instance, enlist your mother in an argument so that she would take their side against you and support their position. Holland continues, "Now, all of a sudden, you're disputing with two individuals, and the chances are not in your favour."

According to Holland, the use of triangulation may prevent manipulative individuals from having to accept blame and can also prevent them from feeling as if they've lost an argument.

Becoming familiar with triangulation might be useful in determining whether or not it is being used. Make it a point to avoid becoming involved in "triangles" whenever they arise out of unfairness.

According to Holland, "this means you're going to have to create and adhere to some tough limits." However, it is important to keep in mind that the purpose of boundaries is not to control other people but rather to guarantee that you are still able to have a good connection with them. "Boundaries are not cold and callous; in fact, they are incredibly good for you."

Bombardment with love

Manipulation by excessive attention, in which the target is frequently showered improperly with presents, praises, affection, and time, is known as love bombing.

These things may be excellent, which may make things confused. Love bombing, on the other hand, is when someone gives you an excessive amount of attention, it seems entrancing to you, and it takes up all of your focus.

The four different levels of manipulation

There are four phases of manipulation, although manipulative tendencies are sometimes covert and perhaps impossible to identify.

Flattery. The first step in manipulative behaviour is for the person doing the manipulation to put on an act of kindness, compassion, and helpfulness. "They may appear as if they want to assist you with whatever you need, but in fact, all they are trying to do is obtain what they want from you," Draughn continues. "They may even act like they want to help you with everything you need."

Isolation. Once this stage has been reached, the person who is manipulating you may begin to cut you off from your family and friends. They may make an effort to persuade you that your loved ones do not understand you or are attempting to exert control over you. According to Draughn, the objective is typically to isolate you from other people who may be able to recognize the manipulation.

Devaluing and gaslighting. Someone who manipulates you may attempt to make you feel guilty or confused during the third step of the manipulation process. According to Draughn, the other person may start telling you that you are ungrateful or that you are the cause of their unhappiness. This stage is designed to make you question who you are, your intuition, and the choices you've made up to this point. Draughn continues by saying that at this level, "it may be extremely difficult to break away from the manipulator's power."

Or, it may be violence. At this stage, which is the fourth and last one, the person who is manipulating you may start to threaten you.

According to Draughn, they may threaten to abandon you, injure you, or hurt themselves as a means of maintaining fear in you as a means of keeping you under their control. When someone is trying to control you by using threats as a method of manipulation, it may be extremely challenging to escape their grasp.

Why do some individuals feel the need to manipulate others?
People influence one another for a variety of motives, including the following:

Control. People who manipulate others may be motivated by a need for control or controlling inclinations, both of which have the potential to provide a stimulating experience.

Low self-esteem. A person may manipulate others as a means of protecting themselves from negative feelings about themselves. According to Jason Drake, the primary therapist and owner of Katy Teen & Family Counseling, "People manipulate mostly as a result of a lack of self-confidence or self-esteem." He thinks that it's possible that they don't believe they have the power to achieve what they desire via their efforts alone.

Ego. Someone who manipulates "may believe that they are the brightest and most capable person around, and might use manipulation to feed their ego that they can outsmart others and gain from their efforts," explains Drake. This is a common reason among narcissistic people, and someone who manipulates "may believe that they are the brightest and most capable person around."

Personal gain. These strategies might be used by a manipulative individual to get something valuable to them, such as money, power, or attention.

Avoidance. It's possible that manipulating others might provide a way out of accepting responsibility for one's conduct.

Chapter Six: How To Influence People

For your brain to make judgments quickly and effectively, it often resorts to various mental shortcuts. Because this happens subconsciously, we can't have complete control over our "cognitive biases," which are tendencies that assist us in coping with the outside world and, eventually, surviving in it. However, even though they may have certain useful applications, some of these biases might create problems.

However, the first step toward getting a bit more influence over how your brain and the brains of others form judgements is to simply develop an understanding of the principles that it follows to do so. It's possible that getting to know these three better can help you become more influential with other people.

How to become more influential

1. EXHIBIT A SENSE OF CONFIDENCE TO EARN TRUST

Who is the brain more inclined to trust: a person who has a successful track record but doesn't communicate effectively or someone who has a less successful background but confidently conveys their ideas? The response may not come as a surprise to you. Researchers from Carnegie Mellon recently discovered that people are significantly more likely to trust someone who projects confidence, even if that person does not have a significant track record to show for themselves.

Our brains actively search for indications of confidence if there is a need to make a choice quickly.

The fact that we may not be as skilled at assessing leadership attributes as we would want to be is unsettling, yet the explanation for this shortcoming is easy to comprehend: Our brains actively search for indications of certainty before making a choice, and we have a natural tendency to give more weight to the opinions of individuals who exude assurance. In practice, trustworthiness might be seen as a condensed form of confidence.

Therefore, the more self-assured you are (or even simply appear to be) when you are presenting an idea, the more probable it is that people will believe that it is a trustworthy path of action; deciding to pursue it will seem like less of a risk.

After all, this should be very obvious to you. It's common knowledge that the way we communicate is crucial, yet it's easy to overlook how much our words may shape others' opinions. In many cases, the concept that is ultimately selected is not always the greatest one; rather, it is the one that is given with the most assurance.

2. SOUND UPBEAT

Does how a physician communicates with a patient have any bearing on the likelihood that they will be sued for malpractice? Ground-breaking research discovered that doctors who used a tone that was flippant and indifferent were considerably more likely to have lawsuits made against them than those who used a tone that was empathic. This was the case even when comparing physicians who had similar credentials.

Furthermore, the tone of someone's voice affects how we understand what they are saying in a variety of additional ways. The results of my study into the scientific aspects of the process of selling have shown that the vocal inflexions used by the salesperson are one of the most important indicators of how captivating a prospective client would find a sales presentation.

Researchers refer to this phenomenon as "mood contagion." One of the primary reasons why the tone of voice is so important is because it can impact not only what we believe but also how we feel. For instance, behavioural scientists Roland Neumann and Fritz Strack discovered that when subjects were asked to listen to a speech, they reported feeling more optimistic if the presenter spoke in an upbeat tone as opposed to a sombre one. This was found to be the case regardless of the content of the speech.

Therefore, if you want to influence and convince others, it may be more successful for you to seem optimistic than it would be to talk in a tone that gives the impression that you are trying to warn, criticize, or cajole them.

3. MAKE IT OBVIOUS THAT YOU WILL NEED TO MAKE A CHOICE

There is currently a lot of scientific evidence to imply that individuals make judgments based on the circumstances in which they find themselves, which implies that influencing the decisions of others requires correctly framing their options. And one of the most effective ways to accomplish this is by merely getting them ready to decide for themselves.

Not only does one's tone of voice affect what one thinks, but also how one feels about something. This is one of the primary reasons why the tone of voice is so important.

It is necessary to concentrate someone's attention on the ideas that you would want them to use as the foundation for their decision to prepare their brain to make a choice. For example, a salesman may pose the following question to prospective clients: "Does it make sense that so many firms that are comparable to yours prefer to do business with us because of our customer satisfaction ratings?" A customer is now prepared to make a commitment that is in line with the value they have just reinforced after first considering that question and reflecting on the satisfaction rankings of a potential business partner.

The majority of the research that has been done on how our brains make decisions indicates a pattern that would-be influencers need to keep in mind: how something is given determines how it will be viewed and whether or not it will be acted on. Your influence is likely to increase if you can align the mental shortcuts that affect perception with the activities that you engage in.

www.ingramcontent.com/pod-product-compliance
Lightning Source LLC
LaVergne TN
LVHW050339160826
845677LV00014B/3693

* 9 7 9 8 3 5 1 5 1 1 1 6 0 *